What Will People Think?

A poetic voyage through the menopause,
relationships, communications
and self-awareness.

Vicky Boulton

© Vicky Boulton 2022

Cover illustration: Madeleine Lumley

Publishing partner: Paragon Publishing, Rothersthorpe

The rights of Vicky Boulton to be identified as the author of this work have been asserted by her in accordance with the Copyright, Designs and Patents Act of 1988.

All rights reserved; no part of this publication may be reproduced, stored in a retrieval system, or transmitted in any form or by any means, electronic, mechanical, photocopying, recording or otherwise without the prior written consent of the publisher or a licence permitting copying in the UK issued by the Copyright Licensing Agency Ltd. www.cla.co.uk

ISBN 978-1-78222-921-6

Book design, layout and production management by Into Print
www.intoprint.net

+44 (0)1604 832149

"The minute you start caring about what other people think,
is the minute you stop being yourself."

- Meryl Streep

CONTENTS

Headspace — 9
Scary — 11
Endless chatter — 12
Inner circle — 13
Hormones — 14
Inside — 16
Price — 17
A moment — 18
Insecurities — 19

Questions — 21
What will people think? — 23
The one — 24
Honest — 25
Raw deal — 26
Overthinking — 27
Options — 28
Maybe — 29

Timings — 31
Toxic — 33
She has been — 34
Smart mouth — 35
Loving me — 36
First step — 37
Solitary box — 38
Patterns — 39

Learning — 41

Same boat — 43
Vanity — 44
Twisted — 45
The call — 46
Shade — 47
Look at me — 48
Spirit — 50

Possibilities — 51

Would you? — 53
Him — 54
Breathing space — 55
The holiday — 56
Biggest mistake — 57
Whole — 58
Beautiful eyes — 59
One night — 60

Self-care — 61

Fine — 63
Rise — 64
Enough — 65
3 F's — 66
Respect — 67
Agenda — 68
Best of me — 69

Realisation — 71

Reflective — 73
People pleaser — 74
End of the row — 75
Pulling the rug — 77

Resilient	78
Doing well	79
Broken	80
Doubt	81

Sense — 83

Wasted words	85
Semantics	86
Drama	87
Instinct	88
Judgement	89
Caged	91
Flaky	92
Complicated	93

Acceptance — 95

Cup of tea	97
What it takes	98
Building block	99
Responsibility	100
Validation	101
Stuff	103
Repair	104
Always me	105

Living — 107

Happy ending	109
Small talk	111
Got the t-shirt	112
Messy	113
Ceremony	114
No	115
Just do it	116
Live well	118

Headspace

headspace

Scary

She never used to worry.
Question 'what if.'
Believe the worst,
or think life was risky.
But age is cruel.
The older you get; the fewer years lie in front of you.
The less time there is to make beautiful memories.
And it's this fear that drives caution and restraint.
Making you behave, toe the line and act your age.
But the worry is, by smoothing the edges
and toning down the extremes,
you're left scared, pliable
and a bit less you
than you have a right to be.

Endless chatter

If only she could turn herself off at the mains.
Or failing that, just press a button for mute.
But to cover-up her nerves and discomfort
in new or tricky situations
she always finds herself overcompensating.

No sooner are the introductions uttered,
she launches sniperlike into a diatribe of rubbish.
Her mouth runs wild, mindless chit-chat reins free,
questions ricochet like badly aimed bullets
and an unsteady laugh shatters any hope of calm.

She forgets why she behaves like this.
Believes it's to do with not liking silence
and a need to fill it at any cost.
But really, she wants to be liked. Needs to be remembered.
Even if that memory is just a wish that she would shut up.

Inner circle

You don't know me.
Not really.
Not properly.

Certainly not enough to voice your suggestions
on what I might like to watch,
where I might like to go
and what delights I might like to eat or drink.

So, whilst I remain in awe of your nerve,
your bravado and your urge to share your opinions,
I kindly ask you to keep quiet, hold your thoughts and wait
until I feel comfortable enough
to invite you into the inner circle
where if you ask the right questions,
you will find out soon enough
that being endlessly directed about my own preferences
is very possibly the worst thing you can do.

Hormones

Dear hormones, I've been understanding
and supportive all my life.
But recently you've overstepped the mark,
left me reeling and full of strife.

Am I happy, or am I sad?
Should I laugh, or should I cry?
Do I let you run amok?
Control my emotions until I die?

I decided to experiment,
mark your progress in my head,
But when you messed up my thermometer,
something needed to be said.

I shouted at you in anger,
confirmed that enough was enough,
But my pleas were useless;
it was pointless to call your bluff.

So, I allowed you to remove
words that once I had fondly used.
Names and dates were forgotten,
leaving me unsettled and confused.

Finally, I called in the cavalry,
loaded my weapons for all to see.
But it seems as if you're immune,
to the superpowers of HRT.

With no other armour for protection
and to keep my sanity intact,
I've issued an ultimatum -
hormones, you're officially sacked!

Inside

And there I was, so pleased with myself for locking the doors
and windows to keep the monsters out.
So proud of my own new-found strength and determination
to survive that I committed the ultimate mistake.
Because anyone can secure a property, a house and a home,
but what happens if the intruders, the unwelcome guests,
or the unhelpful voices are already here,
brought in by us innocently,
oblivious of the chaos they would cause?

Price

How much longer do I need to do this?
When can I stop being there for you?
How many times should I hate you for it?
What result do you really want to achieve?
And why must I still pay all these years later
for something that I can barely remember,
but which you are keen I should never forget?

A moment

She was only a moment away from supreme anger.
A moment from absurd laughter,
a moment from pitiful tears,
a moment from uncomprehending joy,
a moment from losing it completely,
a moment from feeling as if her body was on fire,
or worse still overrun with an impossible itch.

She was only a moment away from wondering if this was it?
A moment when the brain fog would overwhelm her,
a moment when she no longer knew anything,
a moment when sense, logic and control disappeared,
a moment when she wondered what would come next,
a moment from more hormonal delights keen to torture her,
And leave her gasping for the reassurance
of a previous normality.

Insecurities

They must be hungry?
Else why do they find me at night
and try to feed from my soul,
sending doubt and worries to burrow
their way into my brain.
I am a good person.
I can do this.
I will make things work.

But devoid of the sanity and order of daylight,
like vampires they enter the bedroom unchallenged
and slowly undo my good works.
I can feel my courage failing.
My intentions weakening.
My strength fading.
As I surrender to the doubts
that want to consume me.

Questions

questions

What will people think?

Words heard as a child, can be hard to forget,
even when you're grown-up, it's easy to regret,
activities left unfinished, great opportunities lost,
as you listened to others, one more line was crossed.
But now I know better, so I chose to ignore,
a phrase that was popular, but not anymore.
Because I really don't care what's in your head.
Opinions and impressions you might have said,
designed to make me doubt everything I can be,
intended to make you think you're better than me.
What will people think is something I can't control.
Instead, I prefer to listen to my heart and my soul.
Be true to myself; fill my world with welcome calm
so no one else's thoughts can ever do me harm.

The one

When someone needs saving
we expect people to step in and help.
Check up on them.
Reassure them.
Listen and provide support.
Answer questions.
And ensure they're OK.

But what about the person doing the saving?
The person willingly offering everything.
Putting their own needs aside,
hiding their own feelings,
because they know what to do.
What words and phrases to use?
What time, effort, love and solace to give?

Have you ever wondered to whom they turn?
The saviours, the volunteers, the heroes.
When their *tank of caring* empties,
and the weight of responsibility
for someone's wellbeing becomes
too heavy for them to carry alone.

Honest

When did we stop being entirely honest?
Sparing people's hurt by diluting the truth.
Preparing little white lies and massaging egos
to avoid upsetting or destroying fragile emotions,
planning what to say to avoid offence and disappointment.

How did we get here?
To a place where people no longer recognise the truth.
It's a falsity that does not serve us well,
or prepare us for a future where
pain and uncertainty lurk around every corner.

My only regret is that I too have grown dishonest.
So experienced at sugar-coating my words for others
that when you asked if I was happy,
my automatic response was to keep the peace,
utter words guaranteed to sooth and reassure.

Rather than tell you what I really felt,
I prepared consolatory knee-jerk phrases,
kind words in the right order,
all the while praying my face
did not betray our greatest lie.

Raw deal

How many nights have I laid awake dreaming of
this moment?
Prayed for something amazing?
Wished for such an ending?
But now I have it, why do I feel nothing?
No relief. No happiness.
Just emptiness. Numbness. Ambivalence.
As if all the joy has been spent waiting,
anticipating, readying myself.
If this is the deal,
then why not tell me?
Better the knowledge upfront than
feeling I've been cheated.

Overthinking

Why did she do it?
Analyse every word, every silence and every mannerism.
Work out every angle, every nuance and every option.
Spy on every call, every email and every message.
Steadfast in her belief that she was right,
and determined to catch him out,
her life took on another identity.
Exhausted by her efforts and with nothing to show for them,
she wept.
Betrayed by her lack of trust and worn down by her paranoia,
he left.

Options

Customer service questionnaires abound,
businesses wanting to know what you think.
Whether it's positive, helpful, critical
or designed to cause the most stink.

So, why when I think it's essential
and might produce a surprising twist,
is the question I most want to answer
strangely absent from the options list.

Of course, there might be controversy,
people thinking it's a step too far,
with London and the Home Counties worried
that society has sanctioned the bizarre.

But honestly, good people of Britain,
as a minority I want to be heard.
Feel my wishes are fully understood
and my preferences comprehensively referred.

So, what exactly is this feisty topic
I've taken to rambling about.
Essentially, when it comes to Christmas
I want the chance to completely opt out.

Maybe?

Maybe it will work out?
Maybe it won't.
Maybe it will feel different?
Maybe it won't.
Maybe it will be a new start?
Maybe it won't.
Maybe it will make you happy?
Maybe it won't.
Maybe it will be painful?
Maybe it won't.
Maybe it will release you?
Maybe it won't.
Maybe it will change you?
Maybe it won't.
Maybe it will be worth it?
Maybe it won't.

In a life lacking in certainty,
you, and you alone, must decide
whether maybe is better,
than doing nothing at all?

Timings

timings

Toxic

She should have known better.
But in the moment, she forgot everything.
The warnings, the hurt and an end so bitter
that she almost didn't survive.
But as she sees him standing in front of her
begging for forgiveness,
eyes pleading for a second chance
I know she will give in,
driven on by a need to feed
a toxic and twisted addiction
that nourishes her warped soul.
So, with not even a backward glance
at what she has, or how hard she has worked to forget,
she is transported to the past
willing to relive memories sweet and breathtaking,
toy with danger and emotions so deep
that even if she wanted to escape,
she couldn't. Not again.
Because she's gone full circle.
Chosen her fate.
Doomed to repeat clichéd mistakes
until her will is finally broken.

She has been

I can tell by your expression that *she* has been.
Emotional.
Oversharing.
Unburdening herself.
Begging for help.
For validation.
Drawing you into her latest drama.
Draining you of energy
and overwhelming you
with her burning need for attention
and to be at its centre
like the star she believes she is.

But smile my friend.
Catch your breath.
Your job is done.
She is gone.
And I am here.
Asking nothing
but to sit beside you
and let the beauty of silence
speak louder than *her* demands
ever can.

Smart mouth

Renowned for her sarcastic quips,
witty put downs and smart retorts,
she found other people's failings and mistakes
more convenient to manage than her own.

So, when tragedy sadly struck,
her response was oddly muted.
clever words became elusive,
seeming clumsy and inappropriate.

With no weapons left in her arsenal,
she let herself embrace fragility.
Surprised by how light she felt,
when she finally let go of her burden.

Loving me

It's not easy to love me.
At best, I am funny, generous and quirky.
At worse, I am prickly, indecisive and angry.
But for years you took the bad with the good.
Showed me that there was hope.
For me.
For us.
For the future.

But as the anxieties built.
Gradually turning a happy idyll
into something less pleasant.
I felt your hesitation.
Saw your reluctance.
Tasted your disappointment.
As you accepted the inevitable
and delivered your logical decision.

But as you left me to deal
with a future I deserved,
I didn't blame you.
I couldn't see another option.
If I'd been tasked with
saving just one of us,
believe me when I say,
it would always have been you.

First step

Until today I just existed.
But now I am really living.
In finally stepping out of the shadows,
doing what once seemed impossible
and discovering my voice,
I find myself in awe.
Bewitched by its unexpected, confident,
smooth and steadied tone.

Solitary box

They handed it over to me,
six sides of well-worn cardboard
marker penned with your surname,
the words 'do not throw away'
and poorly secured with Sellotape
that had long since forgotten
how to be sticky.

Is this everything that's left? Is this everything you were?
There should be something else? There must be
something more?

But as I open it, I am transported to a house
stuffed full of memories and people who I miss.
A seventies styled room in shades of brown and beige,
display cabinets, discreet lamps, blankets
and deep pile carpets.
A room where the contents of this box once resided.
Where you lived. Where you loved and
were loved.

These trinkets and knick-knacks might attest to your life
but they cannot do justice to your absence.
One box does not amount to your worth.
Cannot equal the value of the stories, or memories,
you have left behind.
But, in bringing it finally to those
who most keenly feel your loss,
I know I have been successful in fulfilling your last wish.

Patterns

Excuses, stories and a hesitancy to commit.
Invalid reasons and incoherent sentences.
Trite phrases trotted out, indicate all is not well.
Yet still you avoid saying anything helpful,
hoping your body language and failure to engage
will do the hard work for you.
Why does this seem so familiar?
Can I really have been here before?
As enlightenment dawns, I recognise the signs
of an unwelcome time before us.
The people might have been different.
A situation much less tolerable.
But I distinctly remember playing these games,
as I tried to extricate myself from him.

Learning

learning

Same boat

How foolish to think we are alike?
Allude to us being in the same boat.
As polar opposites, we sail a different ocean.
Both trying to tame the wildness of the storm.

We have never been remotely similar.
Happy to steer our lives in opposite directions.
You prefer to head recklessly into the wind.
Whilst I choose the safety of calmer waters.

But fate decided it was time to intervene.
Successfully balanced confidence and timidity.
Added common sense, resilience and teamwork.
So, together we could navigate around unfamiliar shores.

Vanity

Don't tell yourself it was OK.
Don't make excuses to explain.
Don't believe there wasn't a better choice.
You did what you always did.
Ignored everyone's feelings.
Disregarded sensible opinions.
Preferring your own solution
and to hell with the consequences.

But as you plunder onwards,
eyeing another personal victory.
Don't think we support you.
Don't take our silence as affirmation
that you were right.
Instead keep us close.
Watch us carefully.
Because one day you will falter
and when you do, we will be there,
offering our help, yet still hoping
to hear a long-overdue apology.

Twisted

I know things about you.
I know what you're capable of.
I know what you've done.
I know who you've hurt.

You're not who you pretend to be.
You're not as perfect as you think you are.
You're not someone who can be trusted.
You're not a good person.

But what to do with this information
is a worrying dilemma.
I want to protect others.
Highlight your failings.
Shine a light on your misdemeanours.
But there is a problem…

To say anything will implicate myself,
underline my own deficiencies,
draw attention to weaknesses that needn't be shared.
So, whilst my desire to speak out remains strong.
I must keep quiet, knowing others may not survive
the fallout from my guilty conscience.

The call

You won't call tonight,
or any other night.
We're done.
You're out.
Reached a point of no return.
Thwarted my attempts to bind you to me
and let me down the only way you know how.

I think I always knew.
Believe I always suspected
that when it came to making good
on a lifetime of intentions,
you would always have the winning hand.

Because in all the years I've known you,
I still can't read you,
or predict your moves.
Whatever this is.
Whatever we were.
You have always played
as if you held all the aces.

Shade

Do not pity the seedling which grows up
in the shadows of the mighty oak.
Stop worrying that it may suffer for its shaded position
and struggle to develop and grow.
When obstacles abound and a bright future
seems improbable,
often, it's those who have endured the toughest starts,
faced the hardest battles and had time
to adapt their behaviours,
not only survive, but smash through boundaries
the rest of us cannot even imagine, let alone navigate.
So, before you judge others
for their vastly different beginnings,
look at yourself first, and consider if you
would have come as far.

Look at me!

Watch them preen, pout and show off.
Post intimate details.
Share vacuous thoughts.
Trot out flawed statements
and reveal airbrushed images
too perfect to be real.
And all for attention, validation and money.

See them influence our behaviours.
Spurring us on to
like them,
follow them,
buy from them,
want to be them.

In their shiny, happy world they look down on us,
baffled by our dreariness.
They live to excess.
Destroy self-esteem.
Believe they are right
and refuse to be judged.

We should be watching them.
We should be connecting to them.
We should be mimicking them.
We should be listening to them.

learning

Because what they are offering is everything,
or is it?

When something seems too good to be true
it usually is.
It's not real.
It's manipulation.
It's deadly.
It's an illusion.

So, put down your phone or tablet.
Disconnect from the app.
Spend time away from them.
Spend time with real people.
Spend time with those who love you
Spend time loving yourself.

Because only when you say 'no'
to their hollow promises, will you find
you are worth so much more.
You are perfect as you are.
You are an individual.
You are a winner.

Spirit

They said she was a free spirit.
They were wrong.
Instead of living on the edge
embracing spontaneity and opportunity
she clung to the safety of the precipice.
Terrified of letting go,
of falling and failing
and being discovered
to be just the same
as me
and you.

Possibilities

possibilities

Would you?

Would you be understanding if I told you everything?
Even though it's not important anymore.
Would you hate me if I said that I had lied?
Even though it was to protect you from reality.
Would you still want me if I told you the truth?
Even though I've tried to forget that it happened.
Would you cry if I told you I would leave you?
Even though I could never walk away.
Would you still need me if I said that I'd used you?
Even though I'd hurt myself more because of it.
Would you forgive me for any of this, even though it's true?
But would it make any difference… if I said I still loved you?

Him

She barely knew him.
Had long since forgotten his name.
No longer questioned either his, or her own motives.
Loneliness drew them together.
Once a week.
For an hour.
A delicious 60 minutes
where nothing and no one else mattered,
not her grief,
her disappointment,
or the growing list of regrets.
For 3,600 seconds she could be someone
desirable, brilliant and beautiful.
Someone to be remembered, if only
for a few brief moments of time,
and that, given everything,
was much more than she deserved.

Breathing space

They said she was inquisitive,
but that wasn't strictly true.
She asked questions, not because she cared for the answers,
but to prevent others from requesting information
about her own life and what she'd done.

Faking interest in other people, albeit only briefly,
brought her much needed breathing space.
Time to prepare lies and stories
designed to keep the inquisitors at bay
until she was ready to admit her truth.

The holiday

It will never live up to the hype.
The smiling nameless faces,
blue skies and golden beaches
images tweaked to suggest perfection
where common sense tells us there is none to be found.

But as we haul our baggage, our triumphs and failures,
our battered, bruised and half empty, unfulfilled lives
closer towards this idyllic representation of fun,
relaxation and enjoyment,
I already know that, however intoxicating the promises,
this holiday cannot ever hope to whitewash over the many lies
we both now seem all too keen to hide.

Biggest mistake

What can you do when it hurts so much?
When you long for his love and to yield to his touch
When the past doesn't matter as you're sure he was wrong
But are you convinced the lies have all gone?

If he hurt you once, he's capable of more.
What makes you so certain, why are you so sure?
As you hope all his promises will finally come true.
But it's not easy to forget what you've been through.

I know you want to believe he has changed.
No more plans needing to be hastily rearranged.
As you remap your future far in advance
Do practised liars deserve another chance?

Friends are nervous, worried your happiness won't last.
Hope his cheating behaviours are confined to the past.
Your willingness to forgive is a credit to you.
As your belief in togetherness carries you through.

I'm here for you always, I'll never disappear.
So, my advice is simple and worryingly clear.
Don't give him your heart 'til you're sure it won't break.
Remember the past and your biggest mistake.

Whole

She couldn't shake the feeling she had missed out.
That there was a path she could have taken,
a different destination she needed to visit,
an important person she should have met.

Because that's the thing with choice.
You make decisions every day.
Some are simple.
Others more difficult.
But all the time you trust you're doing it
with the right intentions
and for the best reasons.

Mainly so you won't turn around in years to come
and feel cheated
because you ignored a chance,
didn't reach out and claim something or someone,
who might have changed everything,
and finally filled the hole of disappointment
that gets bigger every year.

Beautiful eyes

If she was younger.
If she wasn't married.
If she was prettier.
If she wasn't so set in her ways.
If she was someone else.
If she wasn't already a bad choice.

   If…

      The pause button.
      The mental block.
      The reality checker.
      The stopper of dreams.
      The reason for not taking chances
      and for leaving so many things undone.

One night

For one night, let me throw off the shackles
of what is proving to be a complicated life.
For one night, let me be a person unburdened
by hurt, pain and regret.
For one night, let me talk about the
beauty of hopes, dreams and happy endings.
For one night, let me be somebody
who's idealistic, innocent and free.
For one night, let me be with someone
who doesn't want everything from me.
For one night, let me rest, recuperate
and remember just how far I've come
to leave behind jagged-edged memories
where bruises, fractures, scars,
the coldness of steel, blue flashing lights
and the soothing words of kind strangers
were all I once knew.

Self-care

self-care

Fine

Such a tiny word.
Just four letters in all.
But why when asked how I am,
does my response
– when analysed –
raise more questions
for me
than it answers?

Rise

Family should not scar you,
or circumstances harm you.
Events need not shape you,
or life disown you.

Your worth is limitless.
Greater than your belief.
Stronger than whatever,
seeks to bring you down.

When you stumble,
feel lost and alone,
I want you to get up,
carry on with grace.

Because there are many,
who have been denied,
    your choice
    your privilege
    your opportunity
        to rise,
            to rebuild
                and to shine.

Enough

You are enough.
Three words to remember,
when you are busy juggling,
flat out managing expectations,
and wondering how you will get through the day.

You cannot be everything to everyone.
Don't punish yourself.
Be kind, know your limits.
Remember your worth,
and stop giving so much of you away.

3 F's

People live their lives,
so differently to mine.
Following strict rules and behaviours,
that might help them win.

My needs are simpler,
you might say, basic.
If there's friendship, food and fun,
you can always count me in.

Respect

I finally understand self-respect.
It's that moment when you look in the mirror
and feel proud and confident.
Grateful for having behaved with honour and dignity
in situations where other, less worthy options,
were easier and more inviting.

self-care

Agenda

Living life,
according to
someone else's ideal,
is exhausting.

Needing to be acknowledged,
wanting them to be proud,
forever seeking approval,
and putting a hold
on your own hopes and dreams,
is like trying on
someone else's clothes…
        and wondering
                why they don't fit.

Best of me

Only now do I understand why
and see what I must do.
In acknowledging that you are not what I need,
cannot ever fill the shoes I hoped you would,
will never be able to love me like I love you,
am I finally able to put myself first,
see the person I can become,
and walk away from someone
who has never deserved the best of me.

Realisation

realisation

Reflective

That moment of realisation when you discover
the things the media told you were important, aren't.
Your body will never be 'beach ready'.
Your clothes will never be 'on trend'.
You don't eat or drink what you should,
or visit the places on a magical list –
and you couldn't care less.

>That moment is precious.
>That minute is pure joy.
>When you know that by staying strong
>and true to yourself you have resisted
>the sway of those with unreasonable influence,
>giving you back all the power.
>So you can finally congratulate the expectant face
>staring back at you in the mirror.

People pleaser

I am not one person, I am many.
I am who you see.
Your partner, your friend,
your sister, your child,
your confidante and your ally.
But I am also so much more.

I am a thinker, a fighter.
A fixer, a destroyer.
A dreamer, a realist.
A giver and a taker.
An angel or a devil.
I am whoever you need.

I am a people pleaser.
I am everything you want.
With no need to remember.
No desire to revert,
to whom
I once was,
when my voice
only spoke
of the truth.

End of the row

To the girl sat alone at the end of the row.
The loner in awe of a popular group.
The person struggling to fit in.
The last to be picked for a team.
The outsider looking through clouded glass.
The one who tried too hard.
Who felt out of place.
Who didn't measure up.
Who wanted more.
Who didn't know where to go,
or how to just be.

Be strong.
Wait your time.
One day the pieces will fit.
You'll be happy in your skin.
Find your purpose.
Identify with your own kind
and be welcomed.
As your differences are accepted,
your soul genuinely loved.
A sign you have found your home.
A place you never want to leave.

realisation

You may wonder how I know this?
Well, the girl sitting alone
unsure how to move along the row
to sit confidently beside her peers
to twinkle brightly
to share her fears
to give her heart
to find her sanctuary
to discover inner peace.
to accept herself
        …used to be me.

Pulling the rug

Surprise hits me first
followed by disbelief and then hurt.
But as the disappointment seeps through my body
I look at your eyes,
gauge your expression.
Marvel at your ability to keep your emotions in check.
Wonder where it went.
How it can have left you with nothing.
Why all those years mean zero
and you felt that pulling the rug
from under me was fair.
After everything I've done,
I expected more.
Wanted at the very least,
some words of comfort,
an indication that your promises
and our days of happiness,
as well as the plans you made
once meant something to you too.

realisation

Resilient

People said she was resilient,
strong, determined and single-minded.
Eminently practical, she was a problem solver,
a fixer, someone to have on your side
and whose loyalty was never in question.
In a crisis she was calm, responsive and organised.
And when fun was on the agenda,
she added her own brand of entertainment
and good humour.

Over the years, she worked hard, made people happy
and to the outside observer, everything was perfect.
But not once did anyone want to see beyond the veneer.
Not once did anyone question what made her tick.
Not once did anyone ask how she was feeling.
So, one day, when she didn't show up,
People worried about their own loss,
Struggled to see how they could go it alone.

They never saw her again. But I did.
Across a crowded park in the heat of summer.
She sat statue-like still on a bench, eyes closed,
face turned upwards to greet the sun.
She looked different.
Calm. Serene. Peaceful. Freer perhaps?
As if by removing responsibility for other people's emotions,
not being forced to play a role in someone else's spectacle
she had released herself to be the person she chose to be.

Doing well

They said he was amazing.
So talented. So special.
Someone to be looked after,
nurtured so his brilliance could continue to burn,
illuminating the way for others
who wanted to join him in the dazzling light.

But what about her?
The one behind the scenes.
The one quietly getting on.
Hiding her own abilities.
Putting him first.
Supporting him so he got his chance,
his moment. His opportunity.

Remember her when you think of him.
Her sacrifice. Her ability to forgo her dreams
whilst his grew out of reach. Out of touch.
With his sign firmly in the ascendant
she set a path in motion
to slip away and start again in a world
where people would naturally say
she was doing really well… considering.

Broken

She was broken.
Worn down by the effort of trying
   to please,
   to love,
   to live,
   to move forwards.
When all she wanted to do
   was stop,
   lie down
   and sleep,
        until the pain passed.
        Until the darkness cleared.
        Until the memories faded.
        Until the voices stopped
   and she felt stronger.
        Ready to fix herself.
        Ready to mobilise herself.
        Ready to plaster on that famous smile
   so, she could face the world
   and do it all over again.

Doubt

I had to do it.
Share enough concerns.
Raise sufficient issues.
Highlight ample incidences
where you would start to doubt his words,
his promises and his integrity.
Because it's not fair he continues
to function normally,
hurting others needlessly,
causing relationships to falter,
lies to be openly traded
and hearts broken.
I couldn't save myself…
he was too strong
too clever, too credible.
But mark my words… I will do everything
in my power to protect you.
Because if I don't do this,
what sort of friend am I?

Sense

sense

Wasted words

I loved you.
But now you are ruining everything.
Laying bare the truth behind your eyes.
Letting me see the real you.
The person you have carefully hidden
behind a façade of lies.
How clever you are.
How powerful you must feel
to have taken me for a fool;
let me believe our shared plans.
and hope for a future
you were never intending to be part of.

Congratulations.
I hope you're proud of yourself.
But now it's time for you to go.
Quit the cruel games and leave,
I need to regroup;
admit that despite my usually accurate intuition,
my legendary fighting talk,
and a need to lash out with clever words,
I never once rumbled you.
I had no idea.
And it's these failings in my myself
that hurt more than your ultimate betrayal.

Semantics

Years ago, she chose what she wanted
and disregarded everything else.
Tears, laughter, joy and pain filled her days and nights
leaving little energy to question or analyse
the wisdom of her decision.
Focused instead on what she had,
she lived her life with smiles
and a projection of sublime happiness.
Prone to exaggerating the truth so
the whole thing sounded better,
she managed to allay her fears.

Decades later, her eyes told a different story.
Dog tired, weary of incentives that promised so much
but delivered nothing of value,
she questioned if the boat had sailed,
remembered a different time, another place
and wondered if hot-headed impulsiveness
had served up its just desserts.
But on dark nights when the truth came calling,
she could not answer without hesitating;
the question that she all too frequently asked.
Was she settled, or did she settle?

Drama

No, I'm not interested.
No, I couldn't care less.
No, I don't need to know.
I am not your friend.
I am not your audience.
I am not willing ears
eager to hear and react to the next episode
of your self-made drama.
I'm too old.
I'm too tired.
I'm too bored
of your need to be in the middle of it all.
A whirring cog in the futile wheel of
mindless nothingness.
Leave me alone.
Keep quiet.
Enjoy the peace.
As you get older, you'll appreciate the
beauty of silence.
the lack of noise.
the space to think.
and one day you might even realise
that you have never been
– nor will ever be –
that important.

Instinct

She didn't know why she reacted like that.
She couldn't understand why she was leaving,
or explain why walking away was the safest option.
She just realised she needed to listen.
Obey a warning that warranted no explanation.
Stop herself from following an ominous path.
Release herself from an unknown fate.
So in finally following her instinct, she is free.
Safe in the knowledge she has a second chance.
An exit from a situation she would have regretted
and an opportunity to avoid something her body
was all too keen to protect her from.

Judgement

Do not judge me for how I look
there are things you cannot see.
Do not judge me for what I say
there's more you need to hear.
Do not judge me for my choices
there are things you do not know.
Do not judge me for my beliefs
there's more to faith than proof.
Do not judge me on my failures
there are daily battles I face.

If you do judge me…
    judge me for my actions.
            For doing something without being asked.
            Giving with no expectation of receiving.
            Kindness when other options were easier.
            White lies that protect.
            Loving without reason.
            Hoping against all odds.
            Connecting without purpose.
            Helping without motive.

If you must judge me…
   remember I am not perfect.
      Have never professed to being anything
      other than flawed.
         A work in progress,
         just like you and everyone else
         who thought they had a right
         to stand in judgement
         without taking the time
         to discover my story.

Caged

She felt suffocated.
Trapped with little room for manoeuvre.
Scrutinised, watched and judged
like an animal in a zoo.
Taunted by those around her,
she was ensnared
not by walls, bars or locked doors,
but by the terrors within.
Voices reminding her of her failings
pointing out how useless she was;
how she'd 'never amount to anything.'
Even now, years later, I will her to escape -
make a run for it, leave it all behind
that restrictive, energy sapping cage
entirely of her own making.

Flaky

For years I compared myself to her
and found I was strangely wanting.
Part of me thought I should be like her;
better, stronger, more perfect
and a touch less paranoid.

But people are not always who we think they are.
Demons live in all of us.
And at a certain time,
under trying conditions
the real person can escape,
force us to confront someone new
who we don't recognise,
and often don't like.

When I saw the real her,
the person behind the mask
shock and anger gave way to disappointment.
Why had I spent so long wanting to be someone
who was flaky, dishonest and scared?
And when even at my lowest ebb,
my value could be measured
to be far greater than hers?

Complicated

I am not who you think I am,
or who I know I could be.
I am irrational, irritable and infuriating.
I wish I could unravel the jumble
of bizarre and disconnected thoughts, dreams and wishes.
Be more eloquent, more normal, more logical.
I know I confuse, baffle and alienate people
Leaving them struggling to keep up.
Wondering why they should bother.
Sometimes I wish that the impression I gave
was increasingly favourable,
more together, less complicated.
And occasionally, late at night when I can't sleep,
I pray that one day,
you might get to like me,
want to spend time with me,
even if you don't
– and never will –
totally get me.

Acceptance

acceptance

Cup of tea

You are not and have never been my favourite person.
For years I've trained myself to look interested,
ask questions and listen carefully to your answers.
I strive to be polite, bite my tongue and choose
to ignore any hurtful remarks that come my way.
It's a performance where the boundaries are clear.
I understand my role and try not to let myself down.
That's why it's a relief to know
that the true wishes in my head,
coupled with the words I want to say,
will never be heard by you.

What it takes

Maybe it's as it should be.
Perhaps that's all she can expect.
Fragments of comfort.
Wisps of possibility.
Fleeting moments when time stops
and she feels things might work out.
Trust her life might be OK,
believe things will turn out better in the end.
But in a lifetime of dashed hopes and dreams
sometimes even the tiniest shift
can be enough...
                    to finally turn the tide.

Building block

Today seems unfair.
We weren't prepared.
Prognosis delivered without emotion.
Feelings crushed by medical jargon.
Words stark and unyielding.
Facts vast and scary.

It will take time.
Endless bloody research
to understand the implications.
Get our heads around options,
put plans on hold.
Face up to change.

As you process it.
No matter what happens
I'll be spurring you on.
Watching you smash obstacles.
Find another path.
Discover an *after*.

What happened today,
may never make sense.
So, instead I decide to see it
as a building block
of a different future
yet to be realised.

Responsibility

Not everything that goes wrong is someone else's fault.
Some situations cannot be tackled
by simply shrugging and looking away.
Your shortcomings and disasters may never be explained.
Popular syndromes or disorders need not apply to you.
Stop making excuses
and bemoaning your lot.

Don't blame your past, parents or friends,
you don't need a convenient scapegoat.
Instead, ACT.
Follow through on promises.
Forgive yourself and others.
Break unhealthy habits and
forge better ones.

But above else, take responsibility.
Accept that stuff sometimes just happens
you can't control everything.
You're not superhuman.
But when you take ownership,
something shifts
and self-esteem will be waiting to welcome you home.

Validation

I despair.
Another vitriolic update.
One more opportunity to experience painful insight
into a world I struggle to recognise, or care about.

But as I watch, others seem keen to be part of your life,
buy into the chatter, albeit at a safe distance.
In a matter of minutes, I observe people becoming
entranced by your self-indulgent rubbish.
Agog at your never-ending assortment of images
As they try to be part of your group.
Fit in.
Feel worthy to be counted
as your friend.

Do they not realise that by commenting and sharing,
they are just adding to the chaos?
Jumbling up logic.
Messing with reason and responsible for leaving
people alienated, broken and confused?
What happened to 'saying nothing?'
Keeping your achievements, thoughts
and aspirations concealed.
Accepting yourself as you are and not
always seeking approval?

acceptance

No wonder the world is skewed.
Had its values turned upside down.
When all the time people clammer to be heard,
show off, overshare and draw others
into a competition where the boundaries are murky.
But most sad of all, is how many of us resort
to having our actions validated by virtual strangers,
measuring our worth by the number of likes.

Stuff

You buy things because you can.
Jewellery, cars, houses and holidays.
An accumulation of material possessions,
of which you are incredibly proud.

You believe the currency of happiness is money,
as you seek to accumulate everything.
That's where we differ.
Where we disagree.
Instead of envying your life…
       I abhor it.

It seems an empty existence.
Because with no time to enjoy it
and no one to share it all with
you will always be *stuff rich*
but *happiness poor*.

Repair

People think she's strong.
    Capable.
    Accomplished.
    Sorted.
    In control.
On a good day, she's all these things
and much more besides.

But occasionally late at night,
when there's no one else around,
    I have watched her
    crawl across the floor,
    picking up the broken threads of her life,
    hopelessly crying and raging,
    as she tries to stitch them
    back together.

Always me

Cards, emails and presents.
Lunches prepared, meals out, trips away.
Permanently listening, hours of advice, counselling.
Staying calm, accessible and giving over and above.
Until today, I accepted the status quo.
Got on with it,
pleased to have you in my life,
certain it was sufficient.

But now I realise it was always me;
doing, saying, being everything
so you could just float in when you wanted
to talk, take and then leave.
How wasteful that, for years, I let you dictate our relationship
remained grateful for the crumbs that fell from your table.
But now I realise by finally refusing to bend to your will,
ignoring the prioritisation of your needs
over those of others and my own,
I have lost nothing, but gained so much more.

Living

living

Happy ending

Stories tell us there's a chance.
Films show us a different way.
People explain how it's possible.
And throughout every challenge,
every setback,
every opportunity,
and every disappointment,
life ensures you have a choice.

In my search for a happy ending
I've taken many paths.
Made endless decisions
and trusted others with my dreams.
But with every step forward
there was another back.
And with every opportunity,
there was heartache.

Until one day
I stopped trying.
Gave up wishing.
Stood still.
Closed my eyes.
Cleared my mind
and breathed deeply
dispelling those annoying doubts.

living

When I looked around,
something had changed.
I was where I needed to be.
In a place that was home
with a person who sat
comfortably beside me,
eager to share
a better life.

Small talk

Life's too short to partake in mindless chat.
Too brief to make endless small talk with strangers.
Too precious to while away hours with acquaintances
I don't care about.

I don't want to bond, feel comfortable, or *shoot the breeze*
with a whole bunch of niceties thrown in,
with you and anyone else I just met.

Polite conversations are for yesterday.
Today is about things and people that matter,
those I love and need in my life.

So, before you open your mouth, think.
Assess your audience and be clever.
I'm not interested in hearing your wisdom.

But if you're still hellbent on spouting irrelevant dialogue,
intent on hearing the rich sounds of your own words,
then stop, move away and find another person to listen.

Got the t-shirt

Every time you speak
it's a competition.
Everything you have done.
Everywhere you have been.
Everyone you have met.

I am exhausted by your desire
to prove yourself
better than me,
wiser than me,
more talented than me.

Every painful sentence I hear
robs me of feeling,
making me despair,
making me uncomfortable,
making me finally snap.

The next thing you try to say
will be your last.
I have a plan.
I have a solution.
I have an ending.

You can keep the t-shirt –
you'll need it
for another audience,
for another performance,
for another place where I am not.

Messy

Nothing fits neatly into a box.
No one behaves as you think they should.
Nothing works out according to plan.
No one loves you as much as you deserve.
Nothing hurts more than disappointment.
No one tells you the whole truth
because life is messy
and hard work may not yield the results you deserve.

But sometimes your entire world can change
and to be happy you must take chances,
make mistakes, lose something
and find a new way of living.

But you can, and will, make it work,
Nothing lasts for ever.
And without pain, you wouldn't recognise joy.
Without darkness, you wouldn't appreciate the light
Without hate, you wouldn't feel love.
So don't give up, keep moving forwards
be yourself, be strong, be faithful, be happy
because your value has never been in question.

Ceremony

There are no winners.
Medals aren't available.
Accolades have been removed.
Prizes won't be offered,
or awards presented.
The Union Jack will not be raised,
nor the national anthem played.

This is not a time for celebration.
An arena for clever wit,
a place to remember,
time to be right,
or an occasion for blame.
The house lights must be dimmed,
there will be no encores.

Instead, it's an opportunity to reassess.
Regroup.
Lick your wounds.
Count your blessings.
Stop fooling yourself.
Vow never to revisit this place
and give yourself permission to begin again.

No

Not maybe, possibly, or let me think about it.
Never probably, hopefully,
or I'll check and come back to you.
With me there's no middle ground.
Nothing ambiguous, or easy to misinterpret.
Grey areas are not an option.
All confusion is removed.
My belief in two letters, just one syllable,
should be clear even for you to understand.
Because when I say no, you have your answer.
That's it.
End of discussion.
I'm done.

Just do it

Have I misread the instructions?
Did I ignore the signs, wander off the path?
Have I shown you up, embarrassed myself?
Made things awkward?
I didn't realise there were expectations.
Ways I must behave.
Things I should and shouldn't do.
People who I needed to like me.
Decisions that should be agreed.
Actions that must be avoided.
But in my failure to acknowledge your rules
I have turbo-charged my life
discovered fun, happiness, a cheeky giggle
and a smile so dangerously wide
that I now admire this version of me.

So, keep your limitations.
Your age-appropriate guidelines
and need to control what you cannot understand.
You can do, be, have or enjoy what you crave.
You and you alone are responsible enough to decide,
My only advice is select well.
Choose to happily live every day,
even if others do not approve – just do it.

living

Buy the car, see the world, eat the cake,
drink coconut water from its shell on a boat in the Caribbean.
Skinny dip in the sea and dance in the rain.
Cut the people out of your life who disapprove,
drain your mood or are just too needy.
Surround yourself with those who light you up
And make you beam unashamed
like a lighthouse on the shore.

Live well

What if tomorrow didn't happen?
What if today was it?
Finito. The end of everything
with no chance to alter anything.

Would I regret what I had not completed,
or resent the things I had done?
Would I wish I had achieved,
learnt, travelled or loved more?

Or would it finally make sense?
Bring stark realisation?
Because I've always accepted
life is precious
and you never know
when it will be too late
to prove to yourself that you lived it well.

Vicky Boulton grew up in North Yorkshire. Fascinated by words, she started writing poetry aged 10 and has no intention of stopping any time soon. She lives with her husband and several dogs, dividing her time between Northamptonshire and the Brecon Beacons.

What Will People Think? is Vicky's second anthology. Her first, *Eighty-Eight*, deals with the joys and disappointments of relationships, love, growing up and getting older.